GOD DID THIS

"My Soul Look Back and Wonder. . ." Copyright 1995

Published by: Evelyn Phosia Holmes

For further contacts, address inquiries to
Evelyn P. Holmes
P.O. Box 612, Allen Park, MI 48101

Library of Congress Catalog Card Number: 96:94072

ISBN: 0-9661321-5-7

Cover Designed by Evelyn P. Holmes
First Printing 1997

Artist: Ms. Halima Cassells
Cass Technical High School
Detroit, Michigan

Thank You, Halima!

Table of Contents

Table of Contents (continued)

Dedication

"My Soul Look Back and Wonder..." is dedicated to my Lord and Savior, Jesus Christ.

In addition, I would like to thank the servants of God whose teachings have richly blessed my life:

Bishop P.A. Brooks, Pastor, New St. Paul Tabernacle, C.O.G.I.C. (Detroit, Michigan)

(The Late) Bishop W.A. Patterson, Pastor, New Jerusalem, C.O.G.I.C. (Detroit, Michigan - Memphis, Tennessee)

Rev. Robert Smith, Jr., Pastor, New Bethel Baptist Church (Detroit, Michigan)

Martha Jean *"The Queen"* Steinberg, Pastor, The Home of Love (Detroit, Michigan)

Rev. Jasper W. Williams, Jr., Pastor, Salem Baptist Church (Atlanta, Georgia)

Special Acknowledgement to Rev. Joseph B. Barlow, Jr., Pastor, Mt. Zion Missionary Baptist Church, Ecorse, Michigan

And to My Family ...
My Mother, Bernice,
My Grandparents, Will and Emma,
and My Sister, Ann.

Introduction

"My Soul Look Back and Wonder. . ." is a compilation of poems
that I began writing at age 16. Most of them were birthed from a
period of agony and despair experienced while growing up and
attempting to discover who I was and to *Whom* I belonged. Therefore,
the overall flavor of this book is somewhat melancholy, but DO NOT
stop reading. There is light at the end of the tunnel, (I promise!)
I am sure that as a child of God, if you take an introspective look
at your life, you will see the miracle that God has manifested in you.
Without hesitation, you will be able to say along with me, "I wouldn't
take nothin for my journey!"

In the stillness of the night, we sit alone with our thoughts. We
recall experiences that have molded, altered, and even devastated our
lives. It is usually not past *joys* that have had a profound effect on
who we are today, but the uphill *battles* that we have endured.

It is the uphill battles that I have learned to appreciate and even
cherish, for they have taught me to pray and seek a more intimate
relationship with The Lord.

And every now and then, as I reminisce of days past, I find myself
smiling - for *"My Soul Look Back and Wonder, How Did I Make It Over?"*

A TRIBUTE TO

MISS MAHALIA JACKSON

The World's Greatest Gospel Singer

She sang pure soul, undiminished. Her great cathedral
voice sprang forth, as if from some unknown, uncharted
source -- and soared.

"I am a sanctified woman," she said. A minister's
daughter, she was "saved" at the age of ten. So she
did not sing the "blues." But the unmistakable beat
was there, the same rhythmic pulse, the joyous hand-
clapping and "answering call."

Mahalia called it "making a joyful noise in praise of
the Lord." "Don't need no microphone," she exulted.
"Just open the windows and the doors and let the sound
pour out."

Mahalia Jackson, the greatest gospel singer of all
time, was one of six children born in a shack on Water
Street, overlooking the Mississippi River in New Orleans.
By the time she was five, Mahalia was singing every Sunday
in her father's church choir.

Her daddy was a waterfront stevedore by day, a part-time
barber by night, and a preacher on weekends. He gave
his flock a sense of dignity and inspiration.

From her earliest teens, Mahalia worked as a maid and
laundress. She dreamed of being a nurse. "But when
the old people weren't home and I'd be scrubbin' the
floor, I'd turn on a Bessie Smith record to make the
work go faster."

Tribute (continued)

Mahalia's rich, deep contralto voice cast a spell
over audiences on four continents. When she sang
"Silent Night" on Denmark's national radio, 20,000
request for copies streamed in. Four times she
packed Carnegie Hall. She sang for four American
presidents -- Truman, Eisenhower, Kennedy, and Johnson.

Mahalia made the migration from New Orleans to Chicago
longing for a place of her own. When she became known
as an international star, she never lost her humble
spirit. Red beans and rice simmering with pigs'
knuckles, french bread buttered and toasted with garlic,
big red oysters from the Gulf of Mexico, red snapper
baked in New Orleans seasoning with plum tomato sauce,
smothered crabs and turtles, pepper grass cooked low
with streak-o-lean; a feast of these foods was what
she'd cook for her friends whenever she was not on the
road.

Active in the civil rights struggle, she found herself
constantly on the move. Mahalia could never understand
how whites who attended her concerts adored her, yet
when she walked into a restaurant or department store,
they would not serve her.

In the early 1960's she felt like a mule put between
the shafts to plow the furrow. She sang her way across
the country, night after night in a different city. The
pace was killing, and in 1962, she seemed to fall apart.
Lew Mendling, her manager, cut the tour short and brought

Tribute (continued)

her home to Chicago. In the hospital, the doctors
discovered she had developed heart trouble. So many
years on the road had strained her too much. Her concert
dates were canceled, and she stayed home all summer to
rest. She kept in touch with Dr. King; "Come down here
to Georgia," he said to her once, but she replied that
she'd never live to get out of jail where most of them
were ending up. Years later, she sang his favorite song
"Precious Lord" at his funeral.

In 1971 Mahalia found herself in a hospital in Germany.
She sang the old gospel songs with a special tenderness.
Then she collapsed on the stage and was rushed to an Army
hospital, gravely ill. The doctors wanted to keep her
there until she was strong enough to return to America.
Mahalia shook her head. She thought she'd have a better
chance of recovery back home. She did not want to die
away from friends.

On Thursday, January 27, 1972, Mahalia died. The news
spread quickly through the city, and then across the
nation. When her pastor said her remains could be seen
at Greater Salem Baptist Church, they came to see her
for the last time. Fifty thousand citizens, black and
white, came. In subzero weather they stood outside the
church in a slow-moving line, waiting to pass Mahalia's
body. The next day, six thousand people attended the
funeral service. Aretha Franklin sang the gospel songs
that Mahalia had taught her. Three days later, New
Orleans was given a chance to pay its' respect to
Mahalia. The governor of Louisiana and the mayor of

Tribute (continued)

New Orleans led fifty thousand citizens in this final
tribute. Then Mahalia was taken to her grave beside
the Mississippi River, not far from Water Street where
she was born. She was home at last.

*"If you never hear me sing no more, Aw, meet me on the
other shore, God's gonna separate the wheat from the
tares, Didn't He say."*

1911-1972

"My Soul Look Back and Wonder . . ."

(Although this phrase is considered by some to be grammatically incorrect, this song was one of her most famous and most often requested)

How I Got Over

(An African-American Spiritual Sang By: Mahalia Jackson)

How I got over, how I got over, you know my soul look back and wonder, how I got over. How I got over, how did I make it over, (comin on over all these years) you know my soul look back and wonder how I got over! Tell me how we got over Lord, I had a mighty hard time comin on over. Tell me how I got over Lord. I been falling and rising all these years, but you know my soul look back and wonder how I made it over! But soon as I can see Jesus, the Man that died for me, the Man that bled and suffered and hung on Calvary. I'm gonna thank Him for how He brought me and I'm gonna thank Him for how He taught me. Thank my God how He kept me, and thank Him cause He never left me. And I'm gonna thank God for old time religion. And I'm gonna thank God for giving me a vision.

9

Song (Continued)

One day I'll join the heavenly choir and I'll sing and
never get tired. Then I'm gonna sing somewhere round God's
alter and I'm gonna shout all my troubles over. You know
I got to thank God, thank Him for being so good to me. How
I made it over, how I made it over, you know my soul look
back and wonder, how did I make it over. I had to cry in
the midnight hour comin on over. Falling and rising all
these years, how did I make it over. I'm gonna wear a
diadem in that New Jerusalem. I'm gonna walk the streets
of gold. I'm gonna view the host in white. We'll be marching
day and night. Comin up from every nation; on our way to the
great coronation. Comin from the north, south, east and west.
On our way to a land of rest. You know I got to thank God,
thank Him for being so good to me. Early this morning, early
this morning, God told His angels, "Touch her in My name,
touch her in My name! I rose this morning! I rose this mornin
I feel like shoutin! I feel like shoutin!

10

"Ah Done Been In

Sorrow's Kitchen

and Ah Done Licked

Out All De Pots"

___ *Zora Neale Hurston*

I'll Never Be Daddy's Little Girl

I'll never be "daddy's little girl" and sit on
daddy's knee. We'll never share long and cozy
talks about the way life used to be.

I'll never be tucked into bed so tight - protected
from all the world. I'll never hear his deep,
strong voice say with pride, "That's daddy's little
girl."

We'll never share an ice-cream or wish upon a moon
beam or make angels in the snow. Oh, how I still
long for his embrace and why, I just don't know.

I'll never know the joy of seeing his face aglow as
I walk down the aisle. I'll never see the tears that
I've heard granddads shed while holding their first
grandchild.

Gold and diamonds, riches and wealth, I would offer it
all to the world; if I could have heard him say just
once, "That's daddy's little girl."

Pray For Me

Pray for me when my burdens get too heavy
to bear, when I'm struggling to hold on,
when there's no one who seems to care.

Pray for me when my heart is bursting with
pain, when I'm lost in the storm, when my
tears fall like rain.

Please pray for me when I'm lonely and
feeling oh so blue. Pray for me. I'm
only human. You've made mistakes too.

Won't you pray for me at midnight and
sometimes throughout the day? Pray for me
as I fumble along this narrow way.

Pray for me, because I'm trusting that soon
I'll make it through, for maybe not today
but one day soon, you'll need someone to
pray for you.

Jucy

Heaven's little gift that never arrived.
Velvet coffee skin, chocolate tootsie
roll eyes. Big round cheeks, soft and
sweet like cotton candy. Flashing a
toothless grin that says all is fine
and dandy.

I longed to read you stories at night,
while tucked so cozy in bed. Oh, why
you never came I just don't know. Was
it something I did or said?

Visions of washing little hands and
kissing little toes still come to me
late at night. Dreams of your voice
saying "mommy" so sweet, gives my heart
pure delight!

I don't question why the world is round,
or how clouds can hold so much rain. I
don't question Einstein's Theory,
Beethoven's gift, or why you never came.

Jucy (continued)

Just know that I waited, and waited,
and waited, and sometimes I even
cried. But you still remained heaven's
little gift. Jucy, you never arrived.

But I still love you as if you were
here, for you are a part of me. And
I'll see you one day; don't cry, be
sweet. We'll meet in Eternity.

14

For Those Who Think My Poems Sad

I would like to write poems about
birds singing merrily, and lovers
walking hand in hand - sharing
intimate and romantic moments.

Truth is, birds are not singing so
merrily anymore, and my next door
neighbor just blew his wife's
brains out.

Could it be that these are not
joyous and carefree days after all?

Especially For You

I wish I could express exactly how I
feel about you, but for some reason,
words won't do what I want them to do.

I thank God for the day He allowed us
to meet. I thank Him for the days that
followed making my life more complete.

I'll always remember the times you made
me laugh when I felt so down. The times
my spirit was lifted - for a true friend
I had finally found.

Words can't explain how much I needed to
hear the kind words you would say. Your
kindness made me realize that tomorrow
could be a brighter day.

16

Especially For You (continued)

I often prayed I would forget about you
and that bright, warm smile. I often
felt I was wasting my feelings on a love
not worthwhile.

Of course I have shed many tears over
something I wished for, but knew could
never be. And I sat up many a lonely
night wishing you were there with me.

How long this will last or when it will
end is impossible for us to foresee.
But when and if it ever does, I hope that
I have made you as happy as you have
made me.

17

Especially For You (continued)

It's impossible to say all of the
things I'm feeling within my heart.
It is now clear to me that a lot of
things were impossible right from
the very start.

I pray the Lord will forgive us. I
know He has been watching from above.
But dear Lord, it was not my intention
to fall in love with someone else's
love.

I'll cherish forever, the moments we
spent years together, and this
experience we have shared will live
in my heart forever.

18

Reprise: Especially For You

How easily we are deceived by truthful
and caring eyes that once looked into
ours so deeply, so tenderly, and
so honestly.

And how easily we are made fools of
by those with bright, warm smiles that
once caused our hearts to flutter.
And now when he smiles, I see only his
vicious and savage-like teeth devouring
his innocent prey.

How easily we so blindly care for others
and blindly allow our hearts to be led
to slaughter. I believe not this world
was meant for me, nor I for it, for I can
no longer be sure.

The End

I told old gloom and doom "get on down the
railroad tracks." I told gloom and doom to
get on down the railroad tracks. Cause don't
nobody want you, when you're sad and blue
like that.

Me and my old dog gonna walk you to the edge
of town. Me and my old dog walkin' you to
the edge of town. Been thinkin' 'bout the
trouble you've caused and I'm 'bout to put
you down.

Don't stand there lookin' ugly, like you ain't
been kicked out befo'. Take yo' bag of gloom
and start steppin' toward the door!

I'm guilty, yes I am, lettin' you stay so
long was a sin. Come on, we've reached a
fork in the road and this is where it ends.

I said good-bye and danced all night - cause
I needed some joy inside my bones. Too much
time already been wasted, broodin' over things
gone wrong. I said, too much time already
been wasted, broodin' over things gone wrong.

Look At What LOVE Has Done To Me!

Jus' look at what LOVE has done to me!
I'm not the same person I used to be.

Jus' look! Look at what LOVE has done
to my heart! Look at the scars, the
wounds I bear. Look! Come closer and
you will see. The sorrow I feel, the
bruises I wear.

Will somebody look at what LOVE has done
to poor me! You know this LOVE ain't
all it's cracked up to be. I've learned
my lesson and now I can rest. Lord knows
I tried. I did my best.

I don't think y'all understand what LOVE
has done to me! Drained me of my tears
and left me in such misery. It has walked
on my emotions and abused my soul - and
that's jus' the half of it. The real pain
will never be told.

Look At What LOVE ... (continued)

Jus' look at what loving and caring has
caused me to be. Jus' look at what a
fool this thing has made of me! And I'm
sho determined to warn others too. It
would have been better had I never begun.

That's why I'm telling you now, when you
see it coming, don't stand there chile ...
RUN! RUN! RUN!

Look at it! There it is, laughing in my
face! I hope you hear me! You better
listen to what I say! It is no respecter
of persons and this you will one day see
too - Cause the Blues it has given to me,
will one day be given to you! Sho nuff be
given to you!

22

And Then There Are Times

There are times when a fading sunset is simply
too beautiful to behold - like the old woman's
hand-sewn patch quilt, each color a symphony
bright and bold.

There are times when my spirit takes flight, and
journeys to destinations my eyes have not
seen - The Alps of Europe, the Mediterranean
Sea, tropical islands an unearthly green.

There are times when city life is magic, with
people hurriedly on their way - "Goodmorning",
I attempt, "Thank you, for holding the door",
but they usually have nothing to say.

There are times when country life beckons me,
with lightning bugs that glow in the dark.
The smell of magnolias and warm ginger bread,
is why country life reigns in my heart.

There are times when I seek the company of
those who are close to my age. But I prefer
the presence of old folks - so full of wisdom
and grace.

There are times when I get a little weary - life
is sometimes hard to bear - Then I'm suddenly
overcome with thanksgiving, for I know there's
a God somewhere.

Miss Emma and Mr. Man

"Mama's" hand-made quilts were a sight
to see. None finer in all the land.
She soothed sore throats and scratched
up knees - she had medicine made in
her hands.

But she and "daddy" rarely spoke to
each other and never together did
they eat. I loved them so much it
almost hurt, but their love sure
troubled me.

Neighbors stood in awe, scratching their
heads - wondering how "daddy's" collards
did grow. They came asking questions,
"why aren't mine this big?" - they knew
Mr. Man would *know*.

And who baked me teacakes whenever I'd
ask - even though she had things to do?
And who told stories about Femley and
Fomley..."come on dogs heeee-ooooo!"?

Miss Emma and Mr. Man (continued)

My grandfather's hair was as white as could
be. It looked like cotton in bloom - He
said "baby, my hair has been white since
age thirty-three, and yours will be the
same real soon."

But "mama" and "daddy" didn't smile at each
other. And I wondered what could the trouble
be. I loved them so much it almost hurt, but
their love sure troubled me.

"Mama" - thank you, for allowing me to "help"
in the kitchen. I must have been a bother
in there. And "daddy" - thank you, for
demonstrating kindness, and teaching me
The Lord's Prayer.

You did the very best that you could do.
You raised my mother well. And she passed
on to me the lessons you taught her and
that's the story that I've tried to tell.

Tell Me Why

Tell me why we do the things we do.
Tell me why men cannot, cannot be
true. Tell me why we fuss and fight
and lie. Tell me why we're afraid
to live *and* afraid to die.

Tell me why it's so hard to find love.
Tell me why it's so hard to find love.

Tell me why disappointments are so hard
to forget. Tell me why tears are so
very, very wet.

Tell me why the sun always comes up and
then goes down. Why, in times of trouble,
friends can't be found.

Tell me why the stars only come out at
night. Tell me why the moon glows so
very bright.

Tell me the mysteries of life and all its'
troubles and woes. Tell me why a baby
is so special to behold.

How many questions have there been?
Sometimes it's hard to recall. But there
is One Who has the answers. He is the
Savior of us all.

Seasons

We met and it was torrid.

We touched and it was cool.

We kissed and it was frigid.

We loved and it was Autumn.

September 3, 1977!!!!!!!!!!!

27

Uncertainty Within

I am one and I am two.

I am me, yet a part of you.

I can see and feel and hear,

but I am not sure that you

are there. I live for me,

and I live for you. I am

one. I am whole. I am me

but I am you!

Winter

The warm midnight air no longer
carresses my body and cradles
me to sleep.

The heat from the glowing sun
no longer mothers the flowers
it birthed. The flowers are
no more.

The green that once surrounded
us, has left its' home empty
and bare.

The sound of life and laughter
and children at play is with us
no more, and all the world is a
cold and empty gray.

29

Just A Feeling

Just a feeling I get whenever I see
birds in flight; whenever I see a
rainbow or stars shining down at
night.

Whenever I hear birds singing in
the trees; whenever I feel the kiss
of a warm summer breeze.

Just a feeling I get whenever I see
a baby crawling on the floor. Oh, to
watch the ocean rushing to the shore!

Just a feeling I get whenever I see
two people so very much in love
whenever I see the moon glowing
from above.

Just a feeling I get as I listen to
the cold north wind blow; whenever I
see a flower blossom or calmly falling
snow.

It truly makes me wonder how all these
things came to be. How the presence of
One is so strongly felt, yet we cannot see.

Not The First Time

This is not the first time that I've
been last - Standing in the background
watching life go pass.

This is not the first time I've had to
settle for second best. No, not the
first time I couldn't be like all the
rest.

This is not the first time I've cried
myself to sleep and thought my feelings
aloud so my mind could gain some peace.

This is not the first time I've carried
this heart heavy and weak. No, not the
first time my soul has yearned for relief.

This, my friends, is not the first time,
for I've suffered these feelings of
despair in the past. This is not the
first time, but it sho will be the last!

31

Trying Times

These are the times that try men souls.
Times filled with sorrows, hatred and
troubles untold.

I have seen my people burdened and in
despair - Depressed, for when they
called on God, it seemed He was not
there.

The light of faith has become difficult
to see and with heavy hearts and clenched
fists we ask "Lord, why hast Thou forsaken
me?"

These times, trying though they are,
shall not be with us long. We must keep
in mind these times come only to make
us strong.

I will always keep my faith no matter
how difficult times may be. I will
always trust and depend on God, until
from my troubles, I am set free!

Pookie

Pookie, no one knew the day or hour
that God would call you home and death
would rest your weary eyes and leave
us here to mourn.

If only you could wake from this white
cold sleep and laugh with us once again!
True, that your slumber is deep so deep,
but deeper by far is our pain!

So, sleep on cousin and take your rest,
until we are all in His kingdom, we pray.
For death is an appointment all must
keep, as sure as night turns to day.

Midnight Blues

Midnight Blues, just as blue as it can
be. Out of work, out of play, ain't
nothin good to me!

Darkness has a way of shaking you through
and through. Oh Heart, be still, these
nights are long, when a love's lost
thought true.

Funny how it don't bother me while it's
early in the day, but when night time
begins to roll around, old blues comes
creeping my way.

"Baby, baby, baby, all I'll ever want
is you." No thank you sir, keep all of
that; your lovin makes me blue.

What's the sense of all this thinking?!
This worry thing can *keep*! So, goodnight
y'all - see you in the morning. I'm going
back to sleep!

"MY

SOUL

LOOK

BACK

AND WONDER . . ."

After The Rain

I can feel a rainbow stretching out
in me - peaceful days, tranquil
nights, boughs bending tenderly.

I've rediscovered the beauty of an
autumn drenched day; crisp, golden
leaves, quiet rolling seas and puddles
in my way.

And there's a kite flying in the air,
so strong and bright and new; and I
love the smell of burning leaves, and
grass covered with dew.

And I can feel a rainbow, a rainbow,
a rainbow sent from above. And I can
feel God's Presence, covering me with love.

The storm is passing over...at last.

35

Deacon PVT. Courtney L. Stanley, Sr.

A good soldier believes in the cause for which
he fights, and is always ready to obey. His
mind is trained, his commitment does not falter
or stray.

He's precise when following orders, because that's
what a good soldier should be - Forsaking self
and everything else to keep our country free.

He must have prayed a lot on those war torn nights,
out there in the trenches alone. But God spared
his life through danger and strife, and allowed
him to return safely home.

Then one day, he left that battlefield and took
up a new shield and sword. Casting away worldly
weaponry and began his fight for the Lord.

36

Deacon, PVT. Courtney L. Stanley, Sr. (continued)

And surely he must have grown weary and longed
for heaven above. Still your light shines on
those whom you've left with memories to cherish
and love.

So, when Jesus decided to call you, He didn't
say private, or deacon, or even son, but I
heard Him say "Servant, you've fought a good
fight, you've finished your course, now well
done!"

Although Deacon Stanley no longer is fighting
with us down here right now; he's gone up to
glory, to his home up yonder, to fight on anyhow!

*II Timothy 2:3 "Thou therefore endure hardness,
as a good soldier of Jesus Christ."*

37

"Friends"

I wish I had a friend like me - someone
I could tell my troubles to. Someone
to listen when I am happy or just plain
feeling blue.

There are so many topics one can choose
to discuss; the weather, politics or just
about anything else. But my "friends"
are a strange and peculiar bunch. They
only talk about themselves.

Aren't friends suppose to be there to lend
a helping hand? Where are the ones I listen
(night and day) to? These rules of "friendship"
I just don't understand!

Tell me how you sit there and not say a
word? I, who walked with you through the
storm and rain? Is your heart made of
stone? Did you suddenly turn deaf? Maybe
I need to review the rules again.

"Friends" (continued)

Just a word of encouragement, just a bit
of advice. Tell me something I need to
hear. "Friend", I listened and listened
when your world was tumbling down, but
in my distress, you are no where near.

Me, Me, Me is your favorite topic of the day.
Who declared you so important? Was there a
news flash I missed somewhere along the way?

"Friend", you're a pretty selfish one, don't
be deceived; the world doesn't revolve around
you. There are others down here who could use
a bit of compassion and someone to tell their
troubles to.

So, I'll rely on this song I learned a long
time ago whenever you become too remiss. I
sing it when I'm lonely or in despair and it
goes something like this:

"What a FRIEND we have in Jesus, all our sins
and griefs to bear. What a privilege to
carry *everything* to God in prayer."

Remembering Ernest Hemingway

Ernie, you may have been right about this
"walking wounded" thing - allowing others
into your life and all the pain that it can
bring.

You just might be on to something that we all
should faithfully do - hold back the feelings
given so freely. Hold back what's inside of
you.

You said it wounds deep, so deep, so deep,
and replaces the joy thought true. You said
it strikes without warning or cause and there's
nothing that we can do.

I think you were right Mr. Hemingway. It's
all very clear at last! Safe is the heart
that is snugly tucked away. Tis true, but
oh, so sad.

40

Accolades to Mayor Coleman A. Young

Thank you - for managing to momentarily distract us from the repetition of our daily lives by becoming the first African-American elected Mayor, of the city of Detroit.

Thank you - for paving the way for Sharon McPhail, Dennis Archer, John Conyers, Arthur Blackwell, and Charles Costa, for it is upon your shoulders that they stand.

Thank you - for rekindling hope out of the ashes of despair in a town that the media and politicians had declared dead.

Thank you - for the aggrandizement of the Mayoral Office because you stood firm, strong and confident in the face of adversity and controversy.

41

Accolades to Mayor Coleman A. Young (continued)

Thank you - for being an example to our children
that they should not succumb to life's challenges
nor to the small minds of mankind that will
annihilate their dreams, but to be all that they
can be.

Thank you - for remembering Black entrepreneurs
and pulling them up the ladder of success along
with you.

Thank you - for refusing to bow down to carefully
orchestrated attacks on your character and
administration that would have caused others to
crumble.

Thank you - for allowing Kenneth Weiner and the
FBI to prove that the best laid plans of both
mice and men sometimes go wrong.

Accolades to Mayor Coleman A. Young (continued)

Thank you - for being able to stand against the wiles of the devil.

Thank you - for realizing that you are not perfect and reminding Bill Bonds that neither is he!

Thank you - for your "mother wit" and political savvy that left many news reporters speechless and in awe.

Thank you - Coleman Alexander Young, for taking time out of your life to give all that you had to give to the City of Detroit!

Thank you - for being a man.

We THANK YOU, and we wish you well!

43

Our Time Has Come

From the scent of wooden churches where we
kneeled and prayed and sang in unexhausting
jubilation, the praises of our Maker.

   ____   Way Over In Beulah Land!

From a father's cry piercing the night as
his son sways to and fro from a big Oak tree.

   ____   So High You Can't Get Over It!

From a mother's moan echoing throughout the
heavens as her child is pulled from the deep
bloody river of hatred and injustice.

   ____   So Low You Can't Get Under It!

From the thousands of aching feet that
marched, kicked, ran, and stood fast for a
victory long overdue for a people yet
misunderstood.

   ____   So Wide You Can't Get Around It!

Run Jesse Run, Run Jesse Run! Our Time Has Come!

Dance

(After A Stevie Wonder Concert)

Everybody dance!
Let your body move!
Let it sway!
Let it slide across the floor!
Everybody dance!
Everybody dance!
Let your body sing!
Let it scream!
Let it shout!
Let it cry out!
Everybody dance!

Let your body soar!
Let it fly!
Set your spirit free!
Everybody dance!
Dance! Dance! Dance!
Everybody dance!

"We were jammin until the
break of dawn!   Nobody
ever told us that we would
be jammin until the break
of dawn!"

Birmingham

I think it was your smile that wooed
me and made my head go crashing to
the ground.

I don't know what or how it happened,
but I let my guard go down!

I think it was the twinkling of those
eyes so bright, your voice made my heart
skip leaps and bounds.

I don't know what or how it happened,
but I let my guard right down!

And though we had just met, it felt like
love at first sight. I couldn't stop
smiling within! Boy, I've been waiting
for you all of my life! What took you
so long and where have you been?!

Chocolate and caramel arms to hold each
other close. Sweet blackberry kisses
by the pound.

Don't ask me how it happened, cause I
don't know! I just let my guard go down!

Birmingham (continued)

Could it have been the moonlit night as
we strolled through the streets alone?
I'll bet it was your lashes, thick,
curly round and round.

That's it y'all! That's when I let my
guard go right on down!

Was it the kindness you showered on me
right from the very start, or was it the
concern you *pretended* to have that stole
and captured my heart?

I let my guard down, chile. It caused me
joy and pain. It won't happen anymore.
I won't let my guard down again.

Like a fool I believed everything you said,
now my smile has been replaced with a
frown; because I took my eyes off of the
road (that was safe) and . . .

I let my guard go right on down! Sho let
my guard right down!

Mandela's Visit

If the measure of a man is not where he stands in moments of comfort and convenience, but how well he endures at times of challenge and controversy, what then can be said about Nelson Mandela? This seventy-one-year-old man has managed to divert our attention away from the monotony of our daily lives and rekindle hope out of the ashes of despair in South Africa. What can be said about a man imprisoned behind the walls of a racist government for twenty-seven years, robbed of his youth, separated from his family, survived inexpressible physical and psychological slavery and indignities at the hands of his captors and yet has emerged to "envy thou not the oppressor, and choose none of his ways." Weak in body, but sustained strength in mind and convictions!

48

Mandela's Visit (continued)

Mr. Mandela has brought to Detroit a much needed sense of love, solidarity and hope for a racial healing throughout the city as well as the world. Hopefully, his visit will remind some and introduce to others, the fact that South Africa's problems are our problems, that we are not free until we are ALL free, and to remember our brothers and sisters in South Africa when we neglect to exercise our rights to vote, obtain an education and take the safety and welfare of our children for granted. I am grateful to those with the vision to bring Nelson Mandela to Detroit and who worked tirelessly to make that dream a reality for all of us to witness and be a part of.

49

Why We Must Vote!

Since the year 1619, when the first African
slaves stepped onto the shores of Jamestown,
Virginia, life for African-Americans has been
a series of unending battles. But if the
inexpressible cruelties of slavery could not
discourage us, the oppositions we now face
will surely fail!

It is our moral obligation to exercise our
right to participate in this decision making
process that affects our lives and the lives
of our children. Far too many tears have been
shed and too much pain and humiliation endured.
We must never forget those who trudged ahead
of us to pave this political road.

When you walk into a voting booth. . . remember
you are voting on behalf of our ancestors.
You are voting on behalf of Emmett Till,
Nelson Mandela, and every Black child whose
hopes, dreams, and future were drowned in the
murky waters of the Mississippi River.

50

Why We Must Vote (continued)

You are voting on behalf of every mother's
sleepless night after standing over a child's
coffin; dazed from the ruthlessness of a
lynch mob's visit.

You are voting because someone, somewhere
stayed on their knees all night long believing
in the power of prayer.

VOTE!   VOTE!   VOTE!

51

I Wouldn't Take Nothin For My Journey

Yes, I made it over the mountains; through
all of the heartaches and pain.

I trudged through lifes' treacherous weather.
I endured the storm and rain.

I walked this journey alone, no friend or
loved one was there. But I knew that I was
in training and this was *my* cross to bear.

I tossed and turned many nights and asked
God, "Why must these burdens be?" When He
didn't move the mountain, He guided me over
it; for His Grace was sufficient for me.

How often I longed to give up and questioned
the suffering God did allow. Even though I
asked the question "How Did I Make It Over?"
I'm so glad I *know* the Answer and I wouldn't
take nothin for my journey now! No, I
wouldn't take nothin for my journey now!

52

"Trusting The Trainer"

Afterthoughts

The word thoroughbred implies thoroughly trained and skilled. The intense and rigorous training of race horses appears severe to the average person. But on that road to becoming "the best" the trainer will put them through arduous workouts and drills to strengthen their minds and bodies. Once the horse has reached that plateau of excellence, all of the trials and tribulations are worth the pain. In the meantime, the horse and trainer have developed an intimate and personal relationship because the horse has learned to TRUST and DEPEND on the Master. As children of God, we share a relationship with our Master that is very similar to that of the horse and trainer.

Briefly, I would like to discuss the horse and his trainer and as I proceed, allow the Holy Spirit to speak to your heart and compare this training with the journey that God has allowed you to experience.

Training a horse is a progressive thing; going from the lowest level to the highest level. But, before we can discuss training, we must learn all we can about the horse.

The horse is a creature that, standing on his hind legs, is almost twice the height of a man. He weighs in some cases, over five times as much as a man and is also over ten times as powerful. He survived the various ice ages, as well as the age of the dinosaurs and volcanoes, and during this time adapted himself to almost every climate and terrain.

He is one of the oldest known animals on earth. His intelligence is based on his ability to survive. His ability to survive is based on how well he can protect himself.

When he becomes frightened or alarmed, his skin and muscles become taut and he raises his head and neck up high and away from the point of danger. Tightening of the skin makes it more difficult for an assailant to bite or claw at him. (*How tough is your skin?*) His head, thrown up and away from the point of danger, insures protection to one of the most vulnerable spots on his body, the poll.

If attacked from the rear, the horse will shift his weight to his front quarters and kick with a machine-gun-like rapidity that, if it did not miss would soon discourage his assailant. If attacked from the side, threatening flank and stomach, he pushes sideways into his attacker, *quickly* crushing him to the ground. If the attack comes from above, the horse will buck violently. As soon as his assailant is thrown to the ground, he will take off with a speed yet unmatched for his size. In other words, he has on the whole armor of protection just as the Apostle Paul encourages us in Ephesians 6:11"put on the whole armor of God, that ye may be able to stand against the wiles of the devil."

It is important that the horse and his master become acquainted as soon after birth as possible. Of course, an older horse can be trained by a system of education; but the older the horse, the greater the problems you will encounter, as many bad habits may be well established.

A young foal that has never been in contact with man (master) looks at him with distrust and inquisitiveness, staying his distance, yet curious enough to come closer. The master must handle him gently but firmly, enclosing his entire body with this arms. He may struggle, but under no circumstances will/should the master allow him to go free while he is still struggling. (*In the midst of a struggle, have you ever felt God's arms wrapped around you?*) Speaking constantly to him with a soft voice, he will finally become subdued and only when he is quiet and receptive should he be allowed a portion of freedom. This makes a great impression on the colt's mind during his entire life. That is, even though he is restricted, no harm came to him. There is a myriad of information that goes into detail about this process, but I'm sure you can surmise what I am attempting to impress upon your heart.

Oh, if only we had horse sense, that we may be able to trust the Master!

Satan specifically states in Job 1:7 that he travels "to and fro in the earth" seeking to destroy. We can rest assured that the devil is not attempting to give us a cold, but he is constantly seeking to destroy God's children. He wants your life! The greater God's calling is for you, the more severe Satan's attacks. And like the horse, we must be prepared to respond, shielded on all sides with the whole armor of God, for we know not from which direction these attacks will come. We emerge from our training sessions of life's ups and downs with a new outlook and a new view. As children in training, we must be willing with a cross on our shoulders, in our minds and hearts to follow Jesus. Such following requires complete surrender, personal knowledge and the acceptance of Jesus. Where He leads, we must be willing to follow. He will lead us in strange places, place upon us difficult and arduous tasks and expect the impossible from us. The hymn has expressed it this way:

"In shady, green pastures, so rich and so sweet, God leads His dear children along; Where the water's cool flow bathes the weary one's feet, God leads His dear children along.

Sometimes on the mount, where the sun shines so bright, God leads His dear children along; sometimes in the valley in the darkest of night, God leads His dear children along."

Often during our training sessions, it is difficult if not impossible for us to see where God is leading and directing us; and because of the severity of some challenges, we absolutely cannot understand how His molding process will create a new, improved, saved and sanctified witness for the Lord.

The despair you are experiencing *today,* is preparing you for a great work *tomorrow.* And like the foal, if we can learn (early) TO TRUST THE MASTER and lean not on our own understanding...

Adversity is a reality that none of us can avoid. We all ask *why* when adversity strikes. Dr. Charles Stanley, Pastor of First Baptist Church in Atlanta, Georgia contends, "as much as we all want to know the answer to the *why* question, it is really not the most significant question. The real question each of us needs to ask is, "How should I respond?"

I don't know the nature of the adversity you are facing at this time. But I do know that if you will allow Him to, God will use this trial to deepen your faith in His faithfulness. He will reveal Himself to you in ways that are afforded Him only in times of difficulty and heartache. I sincerely believe that God waits to use the adversities we are facing to advance our spiritual growth. The Bible gives us plenty of reason to believe that God could erase all adversity from our lives with just a word. But experience tells us He has chosen not to do that. Far more important than our ease, comfort and pleasure is our spiritual growth.

Dr. Stanley also states "Suffering is unavoidable. It comes without warning; it takes us by surprise. It can shatter or strengthen us. It can be the source of great bitterness or abounding joy. It can be the means by which our faith is deepened. The outcome hinges not on the nature or source of our adversity, but on the character and spirit of our response. Our response to adversity will for the most part be determined by our reason for living, our purpose for being on this earth, as we see it.

If you are a child of God whose heart's desire is to see God glorified through you, adversity will not put you down for the count. There will be those initial moments of shock and confusion. But the man or woman who has God's perspective on this life and the life to come will always emerge victorious!"

The story is told of a little clock that began to think about how many times it would have to tick in the year ahead. It turned out that there were 31,536,000 seconds in the year and both a tick and a tock for each. The very thought of it was too much, and the little clock just wailed and gave up. It stopped ticking and tocking right then and there. However, the grandfather clock came along and reminded the little clock that it didn't have to do all thirty-one million at once; just a tick and a tock at a time. Little clock recovered its balance and took a new lease on life. It began ticking faithfully again.

It is the same with us. We don't have to face all our obstacles at one time. Yesterday is behind us, and we can't carry tomorrow's problems until tomorrow. God helps us make it one day and one obstacle at a time. Every new struggle won means new growth, new strength. Faith is not just some doctrine which is believed, it is a whole way of life. It is a daily dependence upon God, walking with Him moment by moment.

I want to say to the reader of this book, HOLD ON and develop an intimate and personal relationship with the Master. No, you will never live a trouble free life. We know that from Job 14:1; "man that is born of a woman is of a few days, and full of trouble." But once you have an awareness of who you are and to *Whom* you belong...in the midst of the storm, you will feel the sustained assurance that *everything* is going to be alright. I'm a living witness and this book is my testimony.

Don't give up on God! HE WILL COME!

GOD BLESS YOU!

59